Purchased with Title 1 Funds
Guilford County Schools

# DISCOVER
# The Renaissance in England

by Vickey Herold

## Table of Contents

| | |
|---|---|
| **Introduction** ............................................. | 2 |
| **Chapter 1** What Was the Renaissance in England? ... | 4 |
| **Chapter 2** What Was Literature Like? ................. | 8 |
| **Chapter 3** What Was England Like? ................... | 12 |
| **Conclusion** ............................................. | 18 |
| **Concept Map** ......................................... | 20 |
| **Glossary** ............................................... | 22 |
| **Index** .................................................. | 24 |

# Introduction

**The Renaissance** was a time in history. The Renaissance was a time for change.

The Renaissance was in **England**.

▲ The Renaissance was in England.

# Words to Know

 England

 explorers

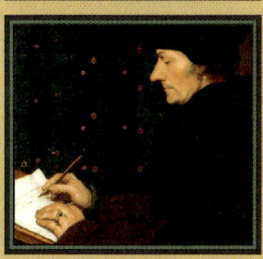 literature

 plays

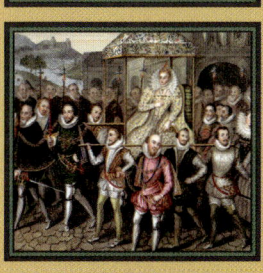 the Renaissance

 theaters

See the Glossary on page 22.

**Chapter 1**

# What Was the Renaissance in England?

The Renaissance was a time in England.

▲ England had the Renaissance.

## It's a Fact

England had the Renaissance from about 1520 A.D.
England had the Renaissance until about 1700 A.D.

The Renaissance was a time to study. The Renaissance was a time to learn.

▲ The Renaissance had learning.

## Chapter 1

The Renaissance was a time for **literature**.

▲ The Renaissance had literature.

The Renaissance was a time for **plays**.

▲ The Renaissance had plays.

## What Was the Renaissance in England?

The Renaissance was a time for kings.

▲ The Renaissance had kings.

The Renaissance was a time for queens.

▲ The Renaissance had queens.

# Chapter 2

# What Was Literature Like?

New writers were in England.

▲ England had new writers.

New books were in England. New books were for the people.

▲ People had new books.

Chapter 2

New plays were in England.

▲ England had new plays.

## Did You Know?

William Shakespeare was in England. Shakespeare was a great writer. Shakespeare was a great writer of plays.

▲ William Shakespeare

What Was Literature Like?

New **theaters** were in England.

▲ England had new theaters.

**Chapter 3**

# What Was England Like?

England had new kings. England had important kings.

▲ Henry VIII was an important king.

England had new queens. England had important queens.

▲ Elizabeth I was an important queen.

## Chapter 3

England had new businesses.

▲ New businesses were in England.

England had rich people.

▲ Rich people were in England.

## What Was England Like?

England had many ships.

▲ Many ships were in England.

England had wars.

▲ Wars were in England.

15

Chapter 3

England had **explorers**.

▲ Explorers were in England.

## What Was England Like?

England had new lands. England had new lands in America.

**Key:** New lands of England

▲ New lands were part of England.

## It's a Fact

Colonists came from England. Colonists came to the Americas. Colonists came in 1607.

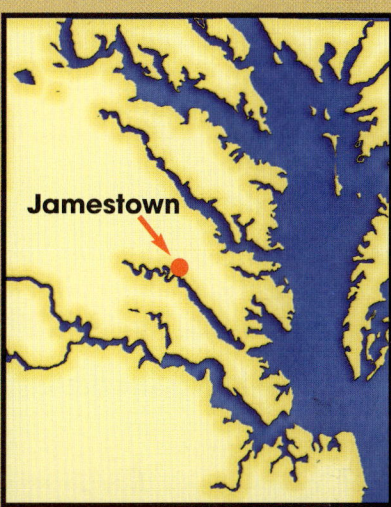

# Conclusion

England had changes. England had new literature. England had the Renaissance.

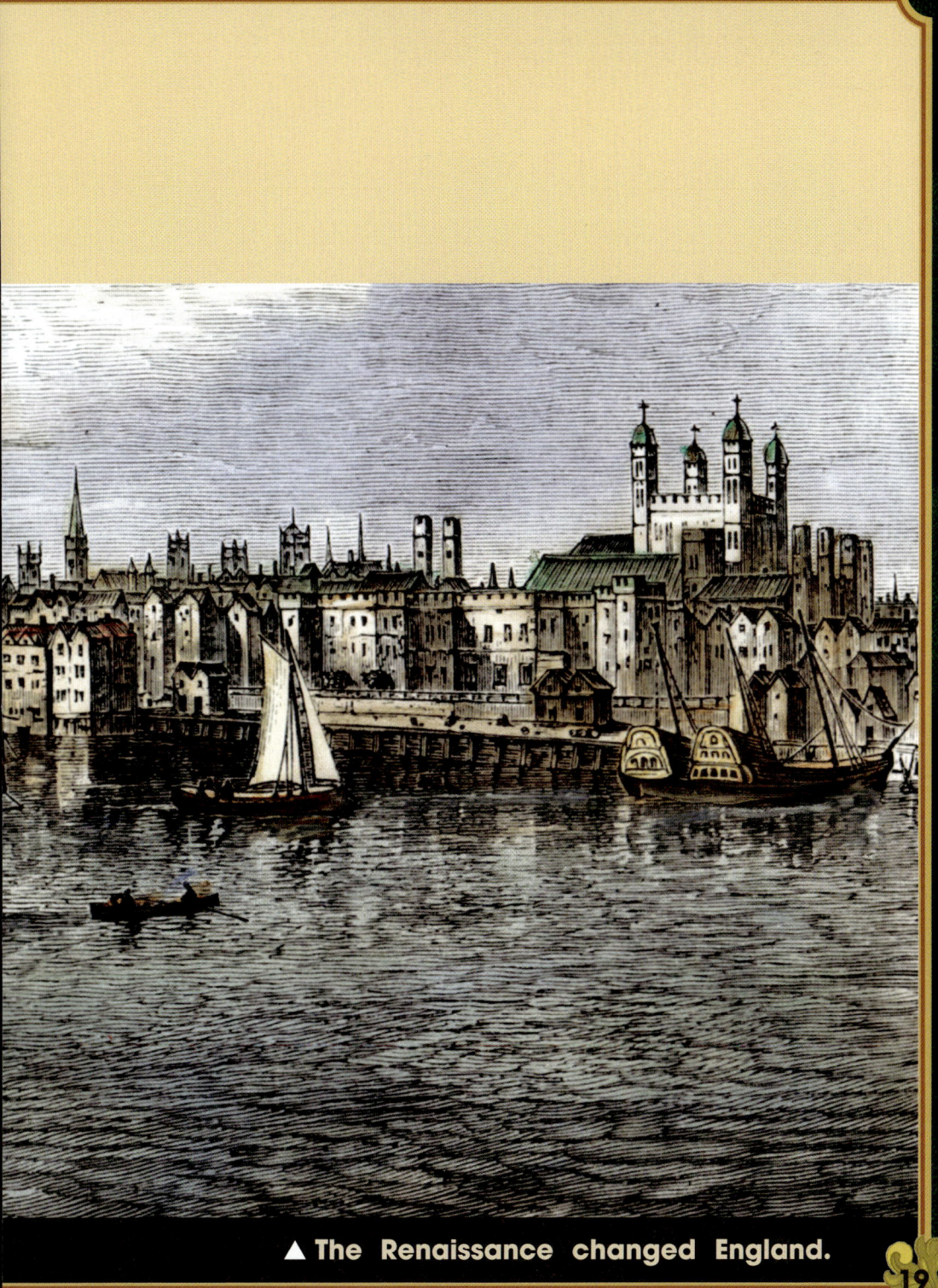
▲ The Renaissance changed England.

# Concept Map

## The Renaissance in England

### What Was the Renaissance in England?

- a time to study
- a time to learn
- a time for literature
- a time for plays
- a time for kings
- a time for queens

### What Was Literature Like?

- had new writers
- had new books
- had new plays
- had new theaters

## What Was England Like?

- had important kings
- had important queens
- had new businesses
- had rich people
- had many ships
- had wars
- had explorers
- had new lands

# Glossary

**England** a country in Europe

*The Renaissance was in **England**.*

**explorers** people who go to new places

*England had **explorers**.*

**literature** written works

*The Renaissance was a time for **literature**.*

**plays** literature performed by actors

*The Renaissance was a time for **plays**.*

**the Renaissance** a time in European history

*The **Renaissance** was a time in history.*

**theaters** buildings for plays

*New **theaters** were in England.*

# Index

America, 17

books, 9

businesses, 14

England, 2, 4, 8–18

explorers, 16

kings, 7, 12

learn, 5

literature, 6, 18

new lands, 17

plays, 6, 10

queens, 7, 13

Renaissance, the, 2, 4–7, 18

rich people, 14

ships, 15

study, 5

theaters, 11

wars, 15

writers, 8